The Reverses of Life

The Reverses of Life

Brian Michael Hurll

To order additional copies of this book, contact:
Xlibris
800-056-3182
www.Xlibrispublishing.co.uk
Orders@Xlibrispublishing.co.uk
781455

CONTENTS

CHAPTER 1
LOVE POEMS

CHAPTER 2
NATURE

CHAPTER 3
TOPICAL

CHAPTER 4

HOME

CHAPTER 5

WAR

CHAPTER 6
TRAVEL

Chapter 1

Love Poems

My English Rose

MY SPECIAL LOVE 1998

I saw this girl across the floor; her softness filled my heart,
Could it be, she's made for me? The thought just made me start.
Love hits you like a hurricane, I don't know what it is,
I only know the thought of her got me in a tizz.
I liked her face, her hair, her smile, the way she held her stance.
And when the tango hit the floor, I thought," She can't half dance"
Her partner swung her this way, then that put on quite a show
I thought again, I can't do that. My morale sank very low.
"Faint heart never won fair lady" I remember being told.
"If you want to make things happen, you must be brave and bold."
I knew that she was beautiful, her bust line firm and full.
Her figure trim and excellent, could I really pull?
I wasn't unattractive, nineteen, not worldly wide.
How do I handle this feeling I have inside?
She looks a bit older, and comfortable in the dance,
I found myself staring, that chassis, I'm almost in a trance.
I pull myself together, is my tie straight, touch my hair,
I look down at my shoes as I get up from my chair.
"Now we'll have a quiet Waltz, get to know each other"
"May I have this dance, please?" I was taught this by my mother.
She smiled, blushed, gave me her hand my arm went round her waist
I turned her to the line of dance, there wasn't any haste.
"Hello, I said, looking down," I've only been here twice"
"Yes, I think I've seen you". She sounded very nice.
She smelt so good; if I could I'd dance the night away.
"I like the Waltz" What is your name?" Mine's Brian by the way"

1

I saw her home, met her mum, we courted for three years,
I bought a ring" Will you marry me, Val?" I love you so much, dear
I've loved her now for forty five years, my family is my life.
I am so glad that Valerie Rose, agreed to be my wife.

Portrait Of A Lady

THE BOOK OF VILLANELLES 1999

A Victorian lady, with a modern feel,
Who radiated love from her house on the hill.
We miss her presence, still, oh so real.
We visited her, she cooked a meal,
So old, no fuss, with culinary skill.
A Victorian lady, with a modern feel.
A Somerset Drawl, a youthful zeal,
So neat, and smart, with a white neck frill.
We miss her presence, still, oh so real.
Her Christian belief, happy to kneel.
Thin, and frail looking, with a very strong will.
A Victorian lady, with a modern feel.
Sharp in the mind, read a good deal,
Content in her little house, close to the mill.
We miss her presence, still, oh so real.
Honest and kind she could never steal,
Now she has gone, her house is cold and still.
A Victorian lady with a modern feel,
We miss her presence still, oh, so real.

THE MIND BEHIND THE FACE 1998

The epitome of kindness, love was all around,
The family adored her, we were on common ground.
My mother's elder sister, Constance Ellen was her name,
A refuge for a troubled soul, she wouldn't claim the fame.
Her hair was curly, dark, and short, bright eyes and fetching specs,
Smart blouse, pearls and ear rings, a credit to her sex,
Womanly, broad minded, wise, consistent, liked some fun.
She made a fuss of everyone, liked her marzipan.
Small in stature, huge in heart, a Christian by her acts,
Understanding, positive, with or without the facts,
So very unassuming delightful in her way,
Admired and respected, more than words can say.
A lady from our working class, untarnished by a war,
Has an aura with her, despite the shortest straw.
Made family life so easy, cared so much for others,
In fact in many ways, she was the queen of busy mothers.
No bad words, a compromise, there is a reason why
A peacemaker, who wouldn't hurt a fly.
Enjoyed life in the country, loved walking in the lanes.
Was happy with a basic life, no fast cars, or planes.
Forgot to tell us she was ill, the news was very bad.
We said goodbye, she passed away, we were very, very sad.
Her memory will never die, the feeling is too strong,
Her name hangs gently on the breeze, like a never ending song.

Missing You

AN EVERLASTING LOVE 2000

From boy to man, I loved you, you were always my guiding light,
That hidden strength, that you'd exude, your inspiration shining bright.
I think of you all so often, I see you so clearly, your smile,
As the years have flown, the pain softens, I'll see you again in a while.
I remember your warmth and your kindness, you always made me feel,
like a man,
I owe you so much, it's hard to express, but I always felt part of your plan.
Its forty long years since we parted, your memory will live in my heart,
I loved you so much, it's uncharted, though you're gone, we are never
apart.
When you left, and went off round the world, I guessed I'd not kiss you
again,
Though older than me, you were my kind of girl, left a void in my heart,
and much pain.
Sorely missed every day, I still see you, in your cosy lounge, by the mill,
Upright and smart, and happy to be, in you own little house, on the hill.
On your birthday we put flowers in a pot, and we talk about things that
we shared,
We loved you a lot, and never forgot, truly special you were, and we cared

How I Hate This World

DEEP WITHIN ME 2001

Oh, how I hate this world, sometimes
It all seems so unfair,
Someone we love, and care about,
confined, to a wheel chair.
She loved the vales of Scotland, most
Met her family, yearly, there,
And now her time is running out,
It does seem so unfair.
She doesn't feel remorse herself,
So happy with her life,
Battling on from dawn 'til dusk
Content, despite her strife.
Oh, how our feelings contrast with life,
Hopes and aspirations dashed,
We wanted a miracle, but in vain,
It seems our world has crashed.
Oh, how I hate this world, sometimes,
We can't give God a dare,
His will, not ours, we must accept,
Makes life seem so unfair
Our hearts will break, we know it,
Our feelings so sincere,
But, others are hurting more than us,
For them we shed our tears.
We hoped, our love would see her through
Our energies we shared.
Let laughter hide our heavy hearts
A sham, so hard to bear.

But we will love this world, again,
Spurred on by thoughts and dreams
Sweet memories of a lovely friend
Because, love wins in the end.

The Joy Of Children

ONLY TIME WILL TELL 2001

I feel so very lucky, having a girl and a boy,
I watched the miracle of birth,
It gave me so much joy.
Wherever my kids were, I was.
They are the world to me.
I wanted the very best for them,
If, that could ever be.
My wife was very patient,
a proper little mummy.
I knew she'd be a wonder mum
When I saw, her big round tummy.
They were lovely, when they were so small,
I n their blues, and whites, and pinks,
When I saw the perfection there, it really made me think.
They grew up quick, then crawled, then walked.
Ate and drank and grew and talked.
We taught them, helped them, sang them to sleep
Fed them, bathed them, counted sheep.
Took them to school, played soccer, did sums,
Had birthday parties, with pals and chums.
Scalded them, loved them, kept them warm,
Gave them time, kept them from harm.
Saw them grow into young adults.
Gave them music and dance, but no weird cults.
Watched summer games, dance competitions.
Cricket matches and musical renditions.
Showed them how to have a life,
Make friends, be happy, without any strife,
Now we are friends, close as can be,

With us, with each other, still come round to tea,
Individuals, now, no nonsense or fuss
Both have cars, so they don't need the bus,
Without any training to be good parents,
Our children are normal, that's apparent.

Kissing Love

TO PAUSE A WHILE

Under an Autumn moon, I love you,
As the moon caressed your face
I knew that warmth would stay forever
Nothing could take its place.
I felt your heart beating softly, gazed
At your beauty so divine,
I knew I would love you for evermore,
That your soul and your heart were mine
We kissed, and the world was our oyster,
Your lips were so deliciously sweet,
I wanted to kiss you forever then,
Kissing love, in love, not parting to eat
Kissing unites souls, and tastes and lips,
Perfumes abound, soft breath on your face,
A serious yearning, an ecstatic heart,
No room for others in our intimate space.
My memories stay with me always and ever
The kissing stopped, and my heart was alone,
Your gentle lips haunt me, regrets I have few,
We must renew our Kissing love, or my heart with turn to stone.

Our Duet Of Love

Startling beautiful, my young heart gave a sigh,
The first time I met you, Maria, my music mistress
You put magic in my heart, and music in my eyes.
I never thought I'd feel again, excitement such as this.
I'm fifteen years older, but still quite slim and sleek,
Since my young husband died, I've longed to feel loves kiss.
You stood there, so smart, in this moment of bliss
Music case in hand, and a flush on your cheek
I never thought I'd feel again, excitement such as this.
"Sebastian, come in. Lovely to meet you like this"
"For a tall man you have a good physique
Since my young husband died,. I've been longing for loves kiss.
The grand piano was gleaming, the lid was really high.
You floated across the floor in that very pretty dress
Startlingly beautiful, my young heart gave a sigh.
"This is my music room, where I play Brahms and Lysst."
"Come sit here beside me, my stool, it will not creak"
I never thought I'd feel again, excitement such as this
"You're Sebastian", you said," Mine's Maria, by the by"
Our overture had started, but I felt no mental stress.
You put magic in my heart, and music in my eyes.
You invited me to your music stool, "Come sit here by my side"
I was very close to you, not trying to impress
Startlingly beautiful, my young heart gave a sigh.
I could feel my body trembling, as I was rather shy
I was doomed, but how you felt, I dare not even guess.
You put magic I my heart, and music in my eyes.
We fell in love, that day, words unspoken, we kissed.
We played sweet music together, not needing to speak.
I never thought I'd feel again, excitement such as this,
Since my young husband died, I've been longing for loves kiss.

11

I'd played so many duets with you, before we said goodbye.
I loved you, truly. madly, but we parted, nevertheless.
Startlingly beautiful, my young heart gave a sigh
You put magic in my heart, and music in my eyes

The Dawn Of My Life

A POEM FOR ALL OCCASIONS

The day we met you opened my eyes
I had been blind long enough for sure
The moment I saw your lovely face
I felt rich, and warm, not poor.
Your sparkling eyes enriched my soul
Your laughter haunts my heart
My worldly doubts are gone away
Now I know we'll never be apart.
Thank you my love, for just being you,
And understanding how I feel
I truly love you, want you near
Now my world with you is real.
Sweet Dawn, you are everything to me
Your very presence lights up my life
We are soul mates now my love
Thank you for being my wife
I look forward to my life with you
Being Alfresco, in the fresh cool air
Sharing my world with you, my love
Now that you have laid my soul bare.
I am so happy, my heart it wants to burst
Dawn, please don't ever go away,
You are my love, my wonderful wife
I'll love you forever........and one day.
God Bless You.
Xxxxxxxxxxxxxx

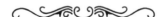

Courage In Adversity

THE CUTTING EDGE 2001

How strong are these people, battling for life?
In pain, suffering, they don't need this strife.
How do they bear it, how do they cope?
Smiling, courageous, when there may be no hope.
Living each day, just carrying on,
Supported by family, where love is strong,
We can't imagine the trauma they feel,
Where, next day is a bonus, the world unreal.
We admire their grit, the will to succeed,
Help them through it, give the love they need.
Support their cause, care, but don't fuss,
Laugh with them listen, give them your trust.
We've all lost family, friends that we loved,
Seen them deteriorate, been hand in glove,
Survival is low, but some battle through,
Fatigued, but happy, to enjoy life anew
A big weight lifted, aspirations now high,
When life is good, not your turn to die,
I raise my hat to their quiet resolve,
It could be me with the problem to solve.

It's A Mystery

BEYOND THE WHISPER 2004

I don't understand what life is about,
It's a mystery, with loads of doubt.
A life begins, too young to know,
Dressed to kill, put on show.
Marmite soldiers, porridge and cake,
Food to eat, a mess to make.
Suddenly you know some stuff
Mum's kind, but Nan's beard is rough,
Things to learn, really quite quick,
Behave yourself, mind the bamboo stick.
Off to school, short trousers, cap
You don't know this is the first lap.
Silly games, hop scotch, and touch
I never liked cold weather much,
Chased the girls, kissed one or two
They were different, not like you
Passed my test, did exams
Went to Weymouth and saw the trams
Suddenly I am in the choir,
They all could sing, but I sang higher
Now I'm someone, have respect.
Discovered girls, went out and necked,
They were different, but smelt so nice,
Would they become my only vice?
Most of my family were women
My best friend died, that's an omen,
I've been happy, then sad
I was sorry, then glad
What does our life really mean?

Weddings and funerals I've seen
Ballroom dancing was next
Hard steps made me vexed
Met a gorgeous girl with charm
Waltzed, held her in my arms
Felt something new, magic
Would this all end up tragic
I had three or four friends
Held hands kissed, no loose ends
This was it, love was real
Something warm, I could feel
Learned how to give,
Learned how to live,
Life is a mystery, living is love
Lost more friends, to heaven above.
Cried buckets, was sad
Had babies, was glad
Miracles happen, life is a yoyo
Sometimes you're up, then you're low
A roller coaster of sadness and joy
Death if a friend, birth of a boy
God wants us to be happy
God invented the dirty nappy
God wants us to know real sadness
Then we'll know real gladness
I'd be dubious if faith was simple
Mystery is like a baby's dimple
I love my friends, I love my life
I love to laugh, I love my wife
Life is a mystery, discover why

Absent Love

LOVE IN INK 2006
CONFESSIONS OF THE HEART 2005

We hardly knew each other,
Yet my heart, it yearns with pain.
We'd shared a few fleeting moments,
But I want you back again.
You were roofing in the valley,
When you saw me in the cart,
Introduced we said a quiet 'hello'
I think I loved you from the start.
Though clumsy and embarrassed,
Special chemistry was there.
An hour before you left to fight,
We touched, kissed, and our hearts laid bare.
I beg you please come home to me.
I am waiting here for you.
I write letters to you everyday,
My love for you is true.
Please stay safe, think of me,
I see your face, hear your voice,
We hardly know each other,
But my heart, it has no choice.
The land can't rest, too much blood.
Our families are all gone.
I dream of you, tears in floods,
As I lay here, all alone.

Those fleeting moments, like tiny diamonds,
Meant all the world to me.
I can't explain how are souls can touch,
So please come home to me.

My Lost Love

SOUTHERN ENGLAND VERSE 2006
THE BEST POEMS AND POETS 2005

How do I cope, give me some hope,
The world seems against me, I only mope
My darling's in heaven, God bless her,
I miss her, I love her, can't cope.
All day I'm busy, working and play,
Something different, every day.
Family visits remind me of her.
I feel like crying, full of dismay.
At night I dream she is with me,
Her laughter sets me free.
When morning breaks I am lonely,
and I wonder where can she be?
My friends are so kind, and I'm grateful,
When I'm busy my life is full.
Then I'm resting, dreaming of her,
So sad, my existence seems so dull.
If I'm honest I long to be with her,
Be close to my love for ever.
As hard as I try, I just want to fly
To her side, to be with her for ever.

Angel Eyes

A TIME TO RHYME 2006

She toddled into my home one day,
Our best Christmas present for many years
She's a gorgeous, curly blond, with big blue eyes
Our granddaughter, we held back the tears
Knee high to a goose, she stands so tall,
My son's daughter, he calls her Ollie
A busy little girl, the world at her feet
We went out and bought her a dolly.
She's nineteen months old, as good as gold
She is now "Our angel eyes"
Her parents have brought her up so well,
She will be gorgeous, clever and wise.
We hope she has a long and happy life,
She comes from that sort of stock.
God willing she will have lots of friends
And peace and love, en block.
We have always loved little children,
Spoilt our own a bit, I suppose.
Angel eyes has come along
We will love her 'til our tired eyes close.
Welcome to our home, sweet little one
We love you lots, you know
Olivia, you give us some happy hours
Nice to meet you, before we go.

Longing For You

A VALENTINE POEM

I remember the first time I saw you,
Being dazed, by your beautiful face.
The feeling was awesome, your sparkling eyes,
Left me dumbstruck, as you passed, with such grace.
I could not miss your feminine curves,
Or the fragrance, of your perfume.
My eyes were glued to your glorious form,
And I realized I was doomed.
My pulse was racing, how helpless I felt
Despairing, that we may never unite.
Thoughts of losing, never knowing your name,
Lost in the shopping crowds, on Friday night.
Now, I am lost in my visions of you.
Imagining names to match what I saw.
Longing to find you, to be lucky, in love.
To hold my angel, who has no flaw.
How can I love you? You are a stranger.
Though my heart is heavy, my hopes are still high
I am sure I could love you. Could you love me?
Could this be real, or pie in the sky.
I dreamt about you, willed you to me,
Tossing and turning, bodies entwined
Awoke, in my ecstasy, calling a name,
Maria, or Marianne, I hope you don't mind.
Five years later we finally met,
We were still single no baggage in sight.
Everything we felt renewing our lives,
Our love was forever, and perfectly right.

Your Sweet Love

SONGS OF HONOUR 2006

I can't bear another day without you,
I never wanted it to be this way.
I miss you more than I could have imagined,
I promise you I never more will stray.
I can't stand another night without you,
I lie awake, wanting you so bad.
I dream about your haunting, sparkling eyes,
I wonder if they still look oh so sad.
I can't imagine another year without you,
Your lovely face haunts me in my sleep.
I tremble when I think of how you hold me,
I remember that your love for me is deep.
I cant wait to hold you close beside me,
To bask again in the splendour of your kiss.
I want to feel your tender arms around me,
And drag me back again, from my dark abyss.
I cant stand another hour without you,
I want your tender lips, touching mine.
The sweet scent of your body, lingering,
And caress your pallid shoulders, so divine

Angels 2008

AWAKENING INSPIRATIONS

There are some angels in this world,
I've met special ones myself.
In fact one took me home with her,
And saved my life, my health.
They come in all shapes and ages,
they lift you when you're down.,
and guide you in their special way
and seldom wear a frown.
They give you hope and private love,
Care for you, and leave their mark.
Discuss, suggest, don't argue
And save you from the dark.
When life gets hard, frustrating,
when troubles pile high.
One angel always finds a way
To let you see the sky.
They've woven wonderful magic,
I'll be forever in their debt
My mother and my darling wife
So lucky that we met
Is there a guardian angel?
Somewhere close at hand
'cos now my mother needs some help,
to take her by the hand.
This world's a strange and difficult place
So unfair in many ways
I love my angels dearly
Let a light shine through the haze

Hope Lives

Son, I told you a small lie years ago,
When you asked me about your dad,
I told you we knew that he would come back
Then when he didn't I was sad.
You see son, it's better to have hoped, and lost
Than to assume he was gone for sure
I knew by your eyes that you hoped as well
but now we'll be for ever poor.
Your dad was a man amongst other men
I loved him so much it hurt
I know he will see how much you hoped
He adored, his little 'squirt'
he would have been so proud of you
he knew you would do well
his hopes for you were truly kept
and yours for him were swell.
hope is a part of a human's life
looking forward to a future bright
keep hoping, son, be positive
and hope will steer you right.
our hopes are powerful, keep us strong,
hope for the best, and plan a course
it is better to hope, and win
these things will god endorse

Chapter 2

Nature

Gods Wonderful World
– A Sonnet

NATURES WONDERS 1999

The wondrous power of a stormy sea,
Wildly whipped crests of breaking waves,
Foamed headed slicks slide up to me,
Sharp sand scurries to a permanent grave.
Volcano erupts, an almighty furore,
Mile high ash clouds, molten lava descends,
Hot, golden river runs, scorching the earth.
Worried inhabitants, glad, when it ends.
A hole appears in a white hatching egg,
A new life breaks forth in a mossy nest.
Solitude reigns, as the morning sun begs
The warmth of the sun, to give people rest.
The wonderful world of Gods good grace,
Miracles of nature control our space.

A Sense Of Peace

WHISPERS FROM WITHIN 2000

I feel a sense of peace, heart felt,
Here in the midst of this dense green belt.
A skylark sings high in the sky
Wispy white clouds, catching my eye
Warm sunny days make your heart melt.
Keeper, carrying a foxes pelt,
Sad, at the hand the dog was dealt
Nature's ecology
Priorities high
I feel a sense of peace.
Crystal River full of salmon smelt,
Summer breeze sways the rising kelp.
Time slipping by, fast as a fly
Quiet and calm, I don't know why.
Whisper a pray, but have not knelt.
I feel a sense of peace

God's Wonderful World

FROM THE LAND OF DREAMS 2000

Albatross flying, in synchronised flight,
Elephant seals winning the chance to mate,
Cheetahs running fast, arriving too late.
Male cat, battle torn, after a hard fight.
Humming birds, nectar charged, wonderful sight,
Gazelles escaping, in flight, they look great.
Some higher power, could this beauty create
Macaws, bee eaters, their colours delight.
Their lives depend on green food and water,
The balance of nature, so important.
Loving care, as a father loves daughter
Important as birds, and insects need plants,
Protection for babes, as the days grow shorter,
Our wonderful world is God's testament

A Sense Of Peace

PASSING EMOTIONS 2000

A skylark sings high in the sky
Wind tipped clouds catching my eye
The warm summer breeze across the vale
As sheep graze gently in the dale
A tiny car moves in the lane,
Just breaking the static view again
The rooks aerobatics, defy the ground
Looping and diving, without a sound.
I feel a wonderful sense of peace,
In this fast world, wonders never cease.
No stress or strain, in this place sublime
The regular echo of the old church chimes.
Peace on earth, a holy quest,
Here, I've found it, I dare suggest,
Maybe this is what I seek,
A hermits existence is not so bleak
Now I'm dreaming of home and wife,
An anchor, to last me all my life.
My beautiful garden, babbling pond
A resting place, of which I'm fond.

Autumn Concerto

THE SKY IS ENDLESS 2004
ETERNAL PORTRAITS 2004

They watched with awe and wonder,
Like spectators in a row,
They bowed their heads and waited
For the dancing, so divine.
There was a gust, a surge of power,
A thousand leaves rose in a swirl,
Leapt thirty feet up in the air,
Light and dainty, like a girl.
The trees applause was rapturous,
They clapped, and bowed their heads, as one,
Green and gold, dancing in the breeze,
Until, the wind was done.
Dancing leaves, they skipped and jumped,
Like a flock of birds on a summer eve.
Then, sank down on their knees.
Autumn in Devon is amazing,
Coloured leaves, and the sheep a-grazing
Reds and golds, browns and greens
Natures way is so upraising.

Natures Dawn 2006

POETRY.COM

The morning sun, popped up from behind the land,
like a huge golden ball, to a new day.
Spreading its warmth, and light, so grand
Changing the view, to a patchwork display.
The wind had dropped, after a breezy night.
From my spot, on the top of the hillock,
I can see nature's widespread delight.
My friends and I, stood, still taking stock
The land was still, the sky getting bright.
From where we stand, the breath taking view,
In all directions, seemed, never ending.
Dawn was breaking, and the day grew.
We never tire, of this panorama, tending
To raise our spirits, for what happens now.
The day gets warmer, the sun higher.
Wispy white clouds, like white fluffy feathers,
Float by, and give us the strange desire
To reach up, and touch them, whether
We could, or not, in this delightful morning scene.
A thin sliver of silver water, still, but moving,
Going somewhere from wherever it's been
Birds start to sing, are they improving?
It's so hard to compare, I've heard them before.
We just stand here, on our little, high hill.
I don't even have to open the door,
We are just three pine trees, up here, standing still.

The Silent Noise

FREE FALLING 2006

I took a deep breath,
As I rested on the side of the hill.
I could almost taste the hay,
Peace and tranquillity.
I gazed up into the heavens.
Pale blue sky with flaky white clouds,
A four engine jet
Making patterns of silver and white
Soaring across the sky
All that power, onwards and upward
The noise totally dissipated by the distance.
At forty thousand feet
Skin temperature minus 35 degrees c
No relativity here,
Peace and quiet.
I hear the screams, see the smoke
As another bomber, commits wasteful suicide,
On a hidden promise.
Smell the death, a huge explosion
My mind has wandered.
No relativity here, in this peaceful place.
The 'baa' of a lamb, finding it's mum
Drifts past my ears, on the breeze.
Loving and caring
The 'pink' of a blue tit
Another 'pink', a twitch of a twig
A flick of her wings and she's gone
The sharp call of a pair of rooks
Renewing their nest in the spring rookery

Soon to be noisy with busy parents,
As they strive to feed their young.
Peace and tranquillity
Only silent noise

An Ode To A Tree

NATURE AT PLAY 2006

I was born here, in this quiet wood
I cannot move, nor would if I could.
I've been here 50 annular rings
And, all the age that those rings bring.
I've seen many others wither and die,
Through damaged limbs and acid skies.
Yet I'm still rooted to my spot
And what a lot of roots I've got.
My canopy is quite large now,
Large enough for rooks and crows.
Plenty of shelter from sun and rain.
The old brown cow is back again.
Now the sun is low and cool,
Trees you know, are no ones fool.
We've had some lovely summer days.
Now we are in to winter ways.
I'm sending my sap back to my roots,
Basically to warm my boots.
My leaves will starve, and turn brown then gold,
Blanket my ground when it turns cold.
Last year I sowed my sycamore seeds,
You might know that even trees have needs,
Hopefully I'll produce some healthy young
I can see some shoots amongst the dung.
I'm quite looking forward to some frost,
To decorate my cobwebs, without any cost
To kill the bugs when the wind blows chill
And the morning mist gives me a thrill.

The ducks are flying in their vees,
To warmer climes, nature decrees.
My branches are almost bare, and cold
Autumn's done as winter unfolds

A Poem For Autumn

POETS FROM SOUTHERN ENGLAND 2007

The long summer days have disappeared,
The evenings are closing in.
Brown, soggy leaves are rotting down,
The winter storms begin.
Let's sing a song for the Autumn glow
The days of glorious shades.
Of gold's and brown's beyond belief
A most spectacular show.
A time to reflect on summer sun,
Of tanned tourists, and sparkling seas
To continually search for shade
Before the fall begins
The evenings cooled, the breeze arose
Helping the trees undress.
A magical carpet beneath our feet
And watch the bare trees pose
Hum a tune for the Autumn moon,
On a sharp clear night, it's white
Enjoy its power and solitude
For the sky will hide it soon.
We all love the changing seasons
From shimmering heat to cold
The interim Autumnal change
Nature planned it, for a reason
And now we await the icy blast,
Of Winter's freezing winds
Of plummeting temperatures, making frost
Until Spring warms us at last.

The Whispering Wind

A BREATH OF FRESH AIR 2007

Today I'm blowing from the cold grey north,
I'm cold and damp, and very harsh.
The spring tide has ebbed beyond the sound,
Flocks of seabirds are feeding on the marsh.
I'm keeping the tide out, so they can wade,
Dig for worms, and hunt shell fish.
I'll give them an hour, cos I need a rest
I don't think that that's too selfish.
From tomorrow, I'll bring some warmer air,
The farms have been busy, the plants need care,
I'll move to the south, produce a warm breeze
And protect the new born lambs I swear.
Sometimes when I think the land is parched
I blow in some rain, a lot at times.
Cover the flood plains, for migrating ducks
When they fly back, from colder climes.
The year the sun will be really warm,
It will drive out the damp and germinate seed.
The wild birds will mate, nurture their young
In tight mossy nests, that they all need
I'll waft in the smell of new mown hay
That will cheer up people and make their day,
I'll take a nap, let the trees grow strong
A barrier from me, when the storms come to stay
All living things enjoy fresh sweet air,
Country folk, farm stock and birds everywhere.
I can help them with that, a gentle breeze
When the sweet sap rises, and souls laid bare.
Sometimes I whisper to the shrubs and trees,

Perhaps you've heard me in the spring
Maybe felt my gentle breath in your hair
I love the seasons, that's my thing.
Nature is fickle, has enormous power,
Sometimes I'm involved in savage storms.
Howling winds, driving torrential rain,
Tearing down trees, destroying forms.
I'm always sad, when I use my force,
I'm a whispering wind, at natures command
Assistance I offer, whenever I can
To animals, plants, even woman and man
I'll always be a whispering wind,
I'll sing through the trees, on a balmy night
Blow the leaves off, when they turn dirty brown
And always be with you, if that's alright

Spreadeagle Hill

My eyes beheld this glorious scene
An intricate pattern of beige and green
Twenty miles of panoramic view
Magnificent greens of every hue
The bright morning sun enhanced the shade
Boundaries of trees of varying grades
Fingers of shrubbery reach for the sky
Feathery hedges, not very high.
Peace and solitude in this static place
No movement or sound of living man
Rambling fields, speckled with white
Those tiny sheep just seem so right.
The land slips away, swiftly and steep
Very strong gradients, like mountain steppes,
Quiet rules this rural sight
A sense of calm in this bright sunlight.
No drifting smoke to spoil the view
Fresh green grass, below sky, so blue,
A huge chasm eroded, from this natural land
Undulating quilt, unspoilt, so grand.

Chapter 3

Topical

The Second Millenium ~ A Disaster

TOWARDS 2000

A thousand years for humans, is but the blinking of an eye,
From dinosaurs and cavemen, to rockets in the sky,
Technology, a modern world, one giant step for mankind,
From quill pens to fountain pens, and guide dogs for the blind.
Two world wars, killing scores, thousands maimed and dying.
Peace at home, but not abroad, some tyrant always trying.
Longbows gone, flintlocks too, chain guns and lasers now,
We haven't learnt a damn thing still, the arsenal grows and grows.
And so do lines of refugees, of every creed and kind.
Ethnic cleansing, genocide, dictators, whole countries mined,
Communications beyond belief, radio, Tv, mobile phones.
Hello to friends, from car and plane, from satellites on their own.
Hello earth, we've landed, we're standing on the moon,
We'll collect some rock samples, be home Friday afternoon.
Word by phone, by telefax, they've sent a drawing through
We can see the man in France we are actually talking to.
Musically the scene has changed, from cylinders to CD'S
Vinyl out, stereo in, the sound is the "bees knees"
From classical, to rock and roll, jungle, techno, rap and soul,
From Woodstock to all night raves, where Ecstasy takes its toll
Multi- cultural countries, brings colours, and creeds together
The world Zest for life, and change, no one can ever tether.
Sexual equality, lesbians, gays, the closet doors are gone,
Moral standards lowered, bondage, AIDS, the list goes on and on.
Cleaner seas, pollution curbed, The earth has had it's summit.
Forests gone, fish stocks down, looks like we'll have to slum it.

Human transplants, hearts and lungs, artificial tickers,
Long queues in the NHS, but none for private pickers.
New source of power, the nuclear age, bombs and power stations,
Let's hope the "Third Millennium" brings peace, to all our nations.

A CALL FROM BEYOND 1998

We were warned about greenhouse gases, but no one took any heed,
Too busy working, making money, there didn't seem any need.
A big ship hit an iceberg, it shouldn't be off Dover,
Apparently others are in its wake, fifty yards wide and over.
The ozone layer has broken up, there's two or three big holes,
The Arctic circle is melting fast, there'll be some heavy tolls.
The gamma rays are getting through, warming up the land,
Suntan blocker ain't no good, it's getting out of hand.
Sea levels are rising every day, two feet more they say,
The landscape's changing drastically, nothing holds the sea at bay
Some coastal roads have disappeared, streams and rivers too,
This is an emergency, someone must help, but who?
Pumping stations are shutting down, contamination rife,
Is this our Armageddon? It's more than a bit of strife.
Tree and shrubs are dying, washed away by the tide,
The homeless head for higher ground, for somewhere safe to hide.
Food and water are getting short, lorries cant get through,
Power gen have warned us, major power failures due.
Radio's working overtime, but time is running out,
This is disaster with a capital 'D', We couldn't handle drought.
Temperatures are soaring, it's 30 degrees in the shade,
People with fast motor boats, doing a ferrying trade.
What will be the end of this, millions of people dying,
Could the world have prevented this? To stem this tide, by trying.
The flotsam is unbelievable, when you reach the waterline,
Wreckage and dead animals, sewage and green slime,
Holland's under water, London underground is dead,
God my body's burning up, It's a dream I'm in my bed.

I'm Really Scared

INTERLUDE OF LIFE 1998

How can this be happening again?
He'd lost so much weight now they've found a lump
Do we really deserve all this pain?
No peace of mind, this could drive you insane,
I feel so awful, I can be such a grump,
How can this be happening again?
We thought we were free, we were going to raise Cain,
Hopes were much higher, now we're down in the dumps,
Do we really deserve all this pain?
We'll have to battle on, through the wind and the rain,
With our friends support, we will pray for a trump,
How this be happening again?
What's left to gain? Is our life down the drain?
Without my husband will I be just a frump?
Do we really deserve all this pain?
We must not panic, I've got to keep sane,
Hope for some good news, that will make my heart jump.
How can this be happening again?
Do we really deserve all this pain.?

Man With No Vision

Meandering Thoughts 1998

What baffles me most on this Earth of ours,
Is, who are these people, in ivory towers,
Whose political views more important than you
And they never listen to our point of view.
Take war torn Africa for a start,
We supply weapons to tear them apart,
Then later when they just survive,
We supply money to keep them alive.
Water's a shortage, that just makes me laugh
The world is covered in it, by more than a half.
It needs purifying, so desalinate it,
Technology's rife; does the world have no wit?
Where there's no water, fit some big pumps,
Irrigate land, plant trees in big clumps,
Fertilise waste land, bring work to the poor,
Open the flood gates, unlock the door.
There must be something, that I've not been told,
The rich have it easier, they're not homeless or cold
We are all equal, so give all a chance.
We can dig tunnels from England to France.
Our climates are changing, the ozone is broke,
So floods in the desert are no longer a joke.
There is work for millions, if the world has a go,
The mind boggles doesn't it, the Sahara with snow?

Coincidence

IN NATURAL HARMONY 1999

Awareness of coincidence is the opening of a door,
A mixture of luck and fate, or maybe, it is more.
It's a link up to our history, a story to be told.
An insight into things to come, a future to unfold.
There is an energy in this world, to most of us unknown,
A molecular vibration, at last the seed is sown.
We've sat upon our laurels, collected material things.
But what on earth are we here for, having everything.
This is almost a religion, the way our lives should be,
Not intimidated or aloof, but filling, growing, see?
Humans, plants need energy, a source of all our lives,
It's not destroyed, just moved around, and everybody thrives.
How can we use this mystique power, given to us to use?
We have to think about it now, or it may be abused.
It's obviously fundamental, transcends basic being,
An insight into spiritual life, another sort of seeing.
Our roots are in our childhood, the way it all began,
To help us understand ourselves, be a better man.
Think of your existence, what does it really mean?
Be un-blinkered, energise, help create our final dreams.

Heathrow Airport

TALES OF OUR TIME 2000

Well, here I am sitting in the middle of Terminal One,
I'm actually working, waiting, but totally free.
The fire bell's ringing above my head,
The announcer said, move or you might end up dead.
There's hundreds of people scurrying about,
It's a busy old place, of that there's no doubt.
Security is hot, so do not leave your bags,
They'll take them away, and turn them to rags.
Do not accept luggage from any stranger,
You could put yourself and others in danger,
It's so very lonely, amongst the crowd
There isn't much noise, no one's talking out loud,
I'm watching the monitor for news of a flight.
The way things are going, I could be all night.
There's cafes and snack bars all over the place,
But the cost of the food takes the smile off your face.
The car park here is over two pounds an hour,
That's only short stay in this concrete tower.
You can spend all your wages, if you park for a week,
The only thing free, is a wash or a leak.
There's dozens of foreigners Asians and whites
Some wear strange head gear, some get uptight.
Others just work here with brushes and cans
Emptying ashtrays or mending the fans.
There are so many signs, directions and such,
It isn't relaxing, I don't like it much.
They're pushing big trolleys, loaded with bags
Waiting for big lifts, stinking of fags.

Search for your car, is it block 'A' OR 'B'
A rotten drive home, too late, for tea.
Give me the south west, down by the coast,
Where it's quieter, and we like it, the most.

A Mini Saga

ONE STEP BEYOND 2001

The princess had always dreamt, that this would happen.
Amazed at the speed of his horse, and the power of his arm,
As he fought his way through the field,--
------she ran out, hoping to meet him.
He dismounted, and introduced himself,
As, Captain James Hewitt, polo player.

POETIC LICENCE 2001

Are we fated to live or die?
Or is it an act of God?
Does it matter if it's truth or lie?
Are we ruled by the rod?
History seems to take it's course
Human conflict does it's worst.
Are we doomed by a magnum force?
Or a huge dam when it bursts.
Our world is a living mass
Earth and wind and fire,
Uncontrollable nature alas,
Producing, a funeral pyre.
Our molten core, geothermal spouts,
Spells a danger of its own
Super magnum having bouts,
Of eruption, to bring us down.
Maybe another Ice age looms,
When the sun, is blotted out.
And ash clouds spill out human doom,
Darkness and cold, no doubt.
So why do we worry about material things?
Destroyed before our eyes,
And if we die beneath molten springs,
That will be no surprise.

The Sounds Of Music

CELEBRATIONS IN VERSE 2001

There's music in an ocean roar,
There's harmony in the air,
There's humming in the beehive
There's singing everywhere.
I've heard the whistle of the wind,
The wailing of the pipes,
I've tapped my feet to drumming,
There are many different types.
Church bells across the meadow,
Are a comforting, easy sound,
The horns of busy traffic,
As, people dash around.
The world is full of music,
Of sounds and rhythmic beats
From dolphins, clicking in the sea
To, a hundred tapping feet.
The trumpet of an elephant,
The squeal of a tiny pig,
The bellow of a farmyard bull
From what I hear, he's big.
What the world needs is harmony,
Friendship and team work,
Nations achieving unison
From this no one should shirk.

It's A Mystery

BEYOND THE WHISPER 2004

I don't understand what life is about,
It's a mystery, with loads of doubt.
A life begins, too young to know,
Dressed to kill, put on show.
Marmite soldiers, porridge and cake,
Food to eat, a mess to make.
Suddenly you know some stuff
Mum's kind, but Nan's beard is rough,
Things to learn, really quite quick,
Behave yourself, mind the bamboo stick.
Off to school, short trousers, cap
You don't know this is the first lap.
Silly games, hop scotch, and touch
I never liked cold weather mush,
Chased the girls, kissed one or two
They were different, not like you
Passed my test, did exams
Went to Weymouth and saw the trams
Suddenly I am in the choir,
They all could sing, but I sang higher
Now I'm someone, have respect.
Discovered girls, went out and necked,
They were different, but smelt so nice,
Would they become my only vice?
Most of my family were women
My best friend died, that's an omen,
I've been happy, then sad
I was sorry, then glad
What does our life really mean?

Weddings and funerals I've seen
Ballroom dancing was next
Hard steps made me vexed
Met a gorgeous girl with charm
Waltzed, held her in my arms
Felt something new, magic
Would this all end up tragic
I had three or four friends
Held hands kissed, no loose ends
This was it, love was real
Something warm, I could feel
Learned how to give,
Learned how to live,
Life is a mystery, living is love
Lost more friends, to heaven above.
Cried buckets, was sad
Had babies, was glad
Miracles happen, life is a yoyo
Sometimes you're up, then you're low
A roller coaster of sadness and joy
Death of a friend, birth of a boy
God wants us to be happy
God invented the dirty nappy
God wants us to know real sadness
Then we'll know real gladness
I'd be dubious if faith was simple
Mystery is like a baby's dimple
I love my friends, I love my life
I love to laugh, I love my wife
Life is a mystery, discover why

This Dangerous World

DANCE WITH REALITY 2001

Those shining towers rose above the Manhattan sky,
A giant tuning fork, for the money we buy.
Standing so proud in a peaceful world,
No one knew what would be unfurled.
What treacherous villainy have we spawned?
What vile hatred on democracy, dawned,
Genocide, theft, destruction and fear,
Wrought by fanatics, which cost so dear.
America stopped, aghast and shaken,
Their proud liberty should never be shaken.
How could this be? Are we at war?
Our world's collapsing, why, what for?
The shock and terror of this vile act,
Thousands, murdered, the Pentagon cracked.
Mayhem and fire in New York streets,
Sorrow, and sadness, courageous feats.
Pandemonium, raining rubble,
Manhattan island has big trouble.
A twisted pile of concrete and steel,
New York's on fire, this can't be real
Terrible images around the globe,
Terrorists invaded our abode.
Stole, our planes, killing our friends,
A vicious enemy can't make amends.
The earth is saddened by this deed,
People of every colour, and creed.
We stand together against shadowy foes,
The net will close on those "sick" heroes.
In the name of any god, this is wrong.

No religion here, on the Devils prong.
How can you sleep, purveyors of death?
Where can you run to, East or West ?
Some one is guilty, some one must pay,
This dirty dog has had his day.
He's bitten off more than he can chew,
Him, and his lethal flying crew.
People of this world unite,
Somehow, we are going to win this fight.
Never again, must terrorism win,
It's evil, sadistic, and a massive sin.
We're miles away from this awful mess,
Our hearts are with you, may God bless.
He'll mend your sorrow, heal your scars,
Unite your families, make them stars.
Those shiny towers must rise again,
A monument to stand, through wind and rain,
A proud democracy, straight and true
A peaceful world, for me and you.

Ode To Mother Earth

INSPIRED MINDS 2010

Is there anyone out there who will listen to me?
My insulations breaking, it's there for all to see.
I'm feeling very poorly, stressed up to my core.
I have an awful feeling my crust won't take much more.
My oil reserves are very low, fossil fuel lacking.
You've drilled so many holes in me everything is cracking.
My inner core is molten, and building pressure fast.
We just had a new tsunami, methinks the die is cast.
My continental plating is effected by the heat,
My atmosphere is warming up, we're all in for a treat
An over load of carbon fumes is killing me for sure
The seas and rivers are tainted, the air no longer pure.
Please help me now, or we will all be doomed
My ecology's unbalanced, I must be groomed.
To let Mother Nature take care of her own
Use my renewable energy, which is well known.
I have wind, waves, and sun, so use them well,
Nurse me, save me and I'll ring like a bell.
We don't want an ice age, famine and drought
Please curb world pollution, and help me out.

Post Millenium

THE WORLD IS YOUR OYSTER 2010

We moved on from our millennium year,
And things are getting worse.
We're suffering a credit crunch,
So there is not much in our purse.
We've been taken to the cleaners,
By first banks, and then the world.
Our government has sucked us dry.
What's next to be unfurled.
Knife crime is on the increase.
Children are being killed
Drug markets seem unstoppable,
And our blood is being spilled

Federal Europe is looming fast,
What's happening cannot be right.
We pay too much, with no return,
It's about time someone saw the light.
Britain is still fighting other wars.
Our soldiers suffering, far from home.
Apparently it's in the name of freedom
But look what happened to Rome.
When it's all about riches, not people.
When greed warps countries minds.
The system then spins out of control,
And we leave this world behind.

A World Crisis

THE END OF DAYS

The world is in crisis, everyone knows.
We've grown mutant superbugs, Our National Health foes.
Flesh eating micro bugs, Carcinoma's are rife,
But individuals don't know, if it's the end of a life.
An unbalanced ecology, is not what Earth needs.
Alien fish are destroying our stock.
Imported, disastrous, ravishing seed.
The Earth's overheating, at an astonishing rate.
One huge supernova will bring the Ice Age,
Darkness and cold will hasten the date.
THE WORLD IS IN CRISIS. The experts know the truth.
The Linchpin Theory will come to pass.
Who's got the courage to show us the proof?
The end of days, into, the end of nights.
Has fate decided, and is it right?
World war three, would dot the "T"
An end to our world, for you, and me.
CAN WE TEMPT FATE, Take a hand?
Water level rising, over coastal sand.
Despots, destroying ethnic race.
Deforestation, increasing the pace.
If there's no way back, we are all at fault.
Financial greed has warped the mind,
Let's just shrug our shoulders and pay the find.
The end of days, God's Promised Land.
Will our Gods allow their followers to fall?
Which faith, which God defends us all?
The seven or eight wonders of the world,
    Destined to perish beneath the force,

Of nature, corrupted by our races
Ecology rebuilt with blood on our faces
Is there a future, is there a key?
Fires can be quenched with a wave from the sea.
Disease can be scorched, so let us see,
If a rebalanced ecology will let us be.
When will it be, someone might know.
If fate takes a hand, then it's time to go
Ask your God, next time you pray,
But are you too late, it might be today.

Gatport Airwick

WHEREVER THE PATH MAY LEAD 2001

Got up early, had breakfast, then paid,
Out, off to Crawley, four hours, we stayed.
Now to the airport, a long, long wait.
Wandered around, got in a state.
Found two soft seats, legs need a rest,
Watched the mad crowd, keeping abreast,
From the high balcony, a panoramic view
A travel message, for me and you.
Incessant noise, and background sound,
The world's worst choir, all around.
No quick movements, just a dull roar,
People talking, pop music, and more.
"Calling passengers, Smith and Wright"
"travelling to Spain" on a now late flight.
A cacophony of sound, blurred and mixed,
A hollow sound, that cannot be fixed.
A million lights of changing hues,
Adverts for perfume, burgers and booze.
Pale blue, and green, now white, and pink.
They seem to change each time I blink.
Pop stars screaming, against the hum,
Some melody, then the beat of drums.
Bing bong, another interlude,
Tell them to shut up, but can't be rude.
Scurrying passengers, spending their dosh,
Some very ordinary, some awfully posh.
Constant movement, just like the planes,
Stairs up and down, then yellow rope chains
Airports never sleep, they've fortunes to keep,

Constant reminders of bargains, to reap.
Odours of beer, then expensive perfumes,
Fast burger bars, a melodic boom,
Tired of mind, can't get no rest,
Awaiting our flight, get back some zest
Now there's some movement, at gate forty seven,
At seven miles high, we're nearer to heaven.
Clear blue skies above white fluffy clouds,
Powering through, away from the crowds.
A large G & T, read some more, of my book,
A hot snack meal, not much to cook.
Now we're descending, it's late evening here,
Through Mahon airport as fast as we could,
At last, we've arrived, the country club's good.

Nine Eleven, Zero One

A VESSEL OF THOUGHTS 2002

This day I saw a fireman cry,
Distraught at loss of friends,
Disbelief engulfed his mind,
His heart would never mend.
Nine eleven zero one,
Will never be forgotten,
The vastness of this callous crime
That shook the world, rotten.
At eight forty six, America stopped,
The deadly deed unfolded,
Now the world retaliates,
The villains badly scalded.
Nine eleven zero one,
The world will remember, ever
Terrorism cannot succeed,
Not ever, never, never.
The coalition does its job,
The Taliban in flight,
Resistance cracking every day
They know they've had a fight.
Nine eleven zero one,
God bless American folk,
The long battle will be won,
The truth, it will be spoke.

Growing Wise

SOMETIMES I WONDER 2004

I wonder now if I am wise,
How wise I am, or wiser.
The more I learned, the less I knew
Questions piled up in the queue,
Like money, for a miser.
I can talk the hind leg off a mule,
Should I think, perhaps listen more?
A still tongue, makes a wise head, fool,
Come down from that tall high stool,
Am I wise, or just a bore?
You have to sit where they have sat,
Are words of wisdom I am sure?
Older now I don't prejudge,
Try and empathise, sift the fudge,
To be wise is to understand more.
I learned to be a listener,
Hear a point of view.
Keep a clear head, sometimes sympathise,
Open up, see truth in the eyes.
Make way for something new.
I've experienced Mexican standoffs,
The next one to speak doesn't win.
Be patient, wait, the answers here on a plate.
Take some action, don't leave it to fate,
Be wise and sharp as a pin.

Contentment

THE TIME AND THE PLACE 2004

A feeling of contentment has come over me,
I'm no longer ambitious or wanting to be.
I have been blessed with a happy life,
Happy, to work for my kids and my wife.
Have had boundless energy, for work and play
Now, I am older I live for today.
I've nothing to prove, that's already done,
I've fought life's battles, and seem to have won.
Blessed with good health, and many good friends,
Will enjoy every day, 'til I come to life's end.
My daughter is happy, what more could I want?
My son has deserted, but was baptised at the font.
My friends are all lovely, loyal and true.
We support one another when someone is blue.
Fate has looked kindly on me, and mine.
Even my fish and canaries are fine.
We have our sadness, and hold memories dear,
Of aunties and uncles, and friends we revere.
A life full of memories, most good, some sad
Strengthened the good, coped, with the bad.
Content in the thought, if I die in my bed
My poetry shows what goes round in my head.
If I be the first to die, be not consumed by sadness.
I was always happy, and would want you to be too.
Please remember me, cos I'll remember you.
Sunny climes and holidays, enrich my soul I know,

As long as I am healthy, I'll always want to go.
Taking nothing in life for granted,
There, but for the grace of God, go I,
I hope you'll know I love you,
Along time before I die.

The Illusion Of Life

EVERY ONE OF US 2004

I have reached a huge conclusion,
My life is an illusion.
It's so vast I can't comprehend.
But I will refuse to pretend,
There is no clue to my past,
Save certificates which cast,
An avenue, to a person's state.
It has dawned on me, far to late.
My past life is made of memories,
Of happenings and long stories,
My future is just hopes and dreams,
Of holidays, and lakes, and streams,
Of places I would like to see,
Of jungles, dense, and redwood trees.
I am not free, don't know my fate.
How long I'll live and have to wait,
Is this the secret of my life?
To procreate, and have a wife,
I don't need an expensive house for this
Relationships and an occasional kiss
This must be a trick of democracy
To comfort me, convince me, I'm free.
Am I a giver or a taker?
I'll have to wait, and ask my maker
Every day of my life is an episode
A variable trip on a windy road
My friends convince me that I'm here, now
Tomorrow may change my life, but how?
If I'm a giver, what have I to give?

Only my life, which I have to live.
If I'm a taker, I get paid for work.
Still get paid, if I decide to shirk,
Whether you're rich, or whether you're poor
you have to stand by the country's law
If you're not bright, or a science boffin
You'll still end up, in a wooden coffin
Therefore our lives are a non event
They came and they eventually went
Your only memory is family, left,
A few possessions, in a cleft.
We live to work, to pay, to eat
Sounds simple, but is no mean feat
Our final gift is a loving thought
Which may be real days
To remind us of this frantic maze,
My life is an illusion, and yours is too.
You know me I might not know you
Stresses build up in the mind
Some people are mean, others are kind
There is no hurry in this life,
It's made up of bits of peace and strife
Random selection must be the key,
What happens next for you and me.

No Return

ETERNAL PORTRAITS 2004

Our life is not a practice run,
We pass this way but once.
Can't turn the clock back, start again,
Restore some excellence.
We feel our way through difficulties,
Mistakes made, but then unknown
It must be luck, that saw us through,
Or fate left us alone.
We are, but pawns in a strategy
To be taken at any time.
Life must be sweet, at any price
'til checkmate is sublime

One Wish

BRITISH ISLES POETS 2006

I have but one wish, for the human race,
That love be law, and war be erased.
Our lovely world is under threat,
From chemicals, we must not let
Industrial waste pollute our air,
Water supplies, and animal lairs.
We need all people worldwide,
To give more love, and be wide eyed
To banish hatred, and religious slant.
There is one God, we take no chance,
If we submit to a common cause,
For peace on earth, and no more wars.
Banish lethal weapons and dynamite,
Let's fight for peace, we have the right
To enjoy, our lives, on limited time.
This is not 'a trial', our world's sublime
We need to care, respect and love
Our families, children, as our Gods love.
Millions wish for peace on earth
They pray, they die, where there's no mirth.
Let's open our hearts, compromise, rejoice,
Because very soon, we will have, no choice.
The world will perish, from lack of care
This is a fact, let the world prepare.
It's not too late, to change the trend
Bring back love, let our Gods attend
To our normal needs, feed and clothe
millions, who suffer where war is loathed.
Fight for the rights, without blood and tears

Walk the street, without any fears
We all desire, to live in an ideal land,
Let conflicts cease, and kindness be grand.
Treat others as you would, your wife
We're only human, and have but one life.
We were not born, to be abused,
The world needs love, and some good news
Let's grant our wish, to one another,
And be kind to some one else's mother.

Brush Up On Your Life

TO SMILE AWAY

You use me every day, you do,
You cannot do without,
In fact, considering my simple style
I do have lots of clout.
You stuff me in your cupboards,
You hang me on the walls,
You use me, then don't wash me off
I don't like that at all
I sometimes get the brush off,
When the carpets need a clean,
But where yards and paths are concerned
I'm the best there's ever been
You use me, to put on paint
You use me on your tiles
I'm excellent at cleaning teeth
To brighten up your smiles
You stick me in your toilets
Which isn't very nice
But when you use me on your hair
You happily pay the price
I smarten up your toe nails
They are often pink or red
And often when you're going out
I do your eyelashes instead
You stick me in all sorts of things
Gooey paint or paste
Then you have to clean me up
Sometimes I'm left to waste
I know, I'm just a silly brush

Made in all shapes and sizes
But I am used by men and girls
From Honululu to Devizes
Sometimes my bristles do fall out
Sometimes my handles break
But you would all be in a mess
If you dumped me by mistake.

What Will They Say

REFLECTIONS THROUGH THE YEAR

The whole point of life, may be hidden from me
But I have my own philosophy
You only get out, what you're prepared to put in
To do less than your best, must be a sin.
Our lives may be controlled, by destiny or fate,
But what will they say, when I stand at the gate?
Will I be known for a villain, or a star?
Have I been kind, and considerate, on par?
Who makes the decision, my God, or my maker
How will he judge me, as a caretaker?
I've done my best, taking care of my life,
Bringing up my children, protecting my wife
Am I destined to be someone unknown?
Will my friends remember, have the right seeds be sown?
Will the world read my poems and understand
That I love my life, and think it grand
What will they say, when I pass away?
Will they remember me kindly for one whole day?
Is it enough, that when my time arrives,
My family will love me for the rest of their lives.
Can I change anything, or is it too late
Is the die cast, has God set a date?
Is love measured on a heavenly scale?
What happens to me, if I falter or fail?

No Daffodils

FAR AND AWAY 2008

I wander, lonely, like a shadow
That flits from wall to wall
When round the corner came rowdy boys
Hundreds of them, shouting, making noise.
In the playground, long corridors, too
Around the back gate, through the trees
A throng of white shirts, and coloured ties,
Shifting endlessly, like grass in a breeze
Around the sporting compounds,
Out, on the playing fields of green.
The boys mingle with the litter
A sight which you all have seen
There are no daffodils around
Too many stamping feet
They've had their laughing heads kicked off
To some pop groups noisy beat

No Time To Waste

IN THE FLIGHT OF FANCY
POEMS 2009

How fragile life is, no time, to borrow.
Here today and gone tomorrow.
No age limit on this rollercoaster ride,
You'd better hope that fate's on your side
When we are young we don't think ahead.
We don't consider tomorrow, we may be dead.
Healthy young bodies and active minds,
Do not mean the world will be kind.
We've no time to waste, it may be our turn
Even if we've got money to burn
The only secret is to enjoy every day
We are all passing through, not here to stay.
Young or very old, we can, only hope to give,
Our kindness to others, whilst we live.
The world has centenarians and little tots,
Those who have a life, and those who'd not.
Have you told anyone, you love them still.
If they're very healthy, or very ill.
Times ticking by, running out for all
Be kind and caring, and walk very tall
How fragile are friendships, and parenthood,
Have we considered, or understood,
That sadness and pain walk every street,
And fate is waiting for someone to meet.

Ode To A Scarecrow 2010

WORDS FROM WITHIN 2010

I am supposed to scare the crows away,
from stripping sown crops apart.
This field is huge, and I'm alone,
Except for the crows, on the cart.
In winter I am stored in a muddy old barn,
And stripped of my clothes, and the dross.
I'm a pile of sticks, collected,
And they call me Driftwood Cross.
In spring I can feel fresh sap rising
When I'm assembled, and dressed to scare
My driftwoods cleaned up, like a shampooed pup
So all fat black crows, beware
I love the warm and sunny days,
I can listen to the natural sounds
But I'll admit I do get very lonely.
It's like being gagged and bound.
I was a bit embarrassed last year.
They cloaked me in a dress.
A great big crow sat on my hat,
And didn't he make a mess.
I don't like the rain, it puts damp in my veins
And raindrops drip from my nose.
My dirty old coat, smells like a goat.
Its from my home in the barn, I suppose.
You see, I can't even scratch my nose.
My arms are sort of long and stiff.
That smell of bacon drifts across

But that's all I get, a whiff.
I wish humans would stop using straw,
Or at least, trim the ends with a knife.
It's prickly, itchy, and uncomfortable,
But it does make me larger than life.

Imminent Danger

SPRING TO LIFE 2012

Our wonderful world is under stress, It is teetering on the brink.

And despite countless threats and warnings, we could become extinct.

We are all in this together, which is easier said than done.

Whilst we at home are reducing power, others consume dirty coal by the tonne.

Our Earth must be getting tired, of bombing, pollution, and us.

Our flora and fauna think they're in a sauna, and we still can't get to work on a bus.

Plants and humans badly need water. Dehydration is not good for our health.

We've gallons of sea water, we need to alter, to provide moisture to go with our wealth.

Wealth is no good without health, our rich Earth needs protection as well.

Boreholes and wells, would remove living hell, and bring up new plants when rain fell.

The time is coming, the oceans are rising. The coast will be changing for sure.

Spring will rise, right up to our eyes, and the reason will not be obscure.

So let us, as a world, change our ways. Please protect what we have got now.

No nuclear bombs, lets fight for our world. Give it back to our children, somehow.

Think of the wonders of nature we'll lose. Our butterflies, flowers and birds.

Let's all make a stand and protect our land. To lose it would be tragically absurd.

Green fields and plants are precious. So are our rivers and seas.

We have the right skills, now we need the strong wills

To mature, and stop industry felling our trees.

Our happiness is at stake, it's a partnership, between nature, and the human race.

Nature will win, and throw us in the bin, if we don't compromise, with good grace.

In less than one lifetime, there may be no one left to read this

The Ramrod 2006

You think that people, don't know who you are ?
You've done some stuff, it left a scar.
Images flash in your mind,
You think they see, you've been unkind.
Hiding, behind a 'pleasant 'mask.
Is it a strain, and not an easy task?
Ten years on, you didn't know that she was wed,
Didn't say, that her husband had fled.
You don't know people, they don't know you.
You worry too much, they haven't a clue
How they see you is, here and now
Kind and gentle, a worried brow,
Thoughtful, not what you were,
Things, all happening, in a blur.
Just seeking justice like a man,
Steady, determined, working a plan
What she sees, is a man with hope
Who she sees can really cope
Sees the feeling in your eyes
Senses what you can't disguise
Hoping you'll stay, and make a life
Hoping you'll take her to be your wife.
Leaving you free to make a choice
Stutter your feelings with trembling voice
"I'm not who you think, I have no home"
"If I had you, I would not roam"

"The thought of never seeing your face"
"never to see your feminine grace"
"I have to go, but I'll return soon"
"I think I loved you from the first noon"

Chapter 4

Home

Background

TURNING TIDES 1998
THE SLEEPING WINDS 1998

Sometimes I sit and listen, without the radio on,
At background sounds around me, that just go on, and on.
The gas valve opens with a click, our boiler springs to life,
The village clock strikes ten o'clock, in the church I wed my wife.
Rain drops on the window ledge, a sharp, but homely sound,
The clock ticks on the kitchen wall, as its hands go round, and round.
The compressor on the fridge cuts in, there's that quiet hum again,
Across the fields, towards the moors, the faint rumble of a train.
A front gate creaks, an engine starts, there are tyres on the road.
From my chair, a cacophony of sound around my small abode.
A police siren getting louder, a distant aircraft hum,
Footsteps on the garden path, at last the mail has come.
I realise sounds are different, now, from nineteen forty three,
The gas lamps hissing in the rooms, windows rattling free.
Not so much a traffic roar, more the occasional motor bike.
Endless freight trains, rattling past, not pretty sight.
All these sounds bring memories, of the past and loved ones gone.
My background sounds, in future, will just go on, and on.
A sparrow chirps, a pine tree groans, contrasting with a horn.
The doorbell rings, a cuckoo sings, I'm glad that I was born.

Auto Obituary

HERE LIES 1998

I remember those days when I was lad,
We'd just survived war, and things were bad,
I loved my life, my children, my wife,
Pardon the pun, but they were 'all my life'
Please don't mourn, 'because I'm glad I was born,
Remember the laughter, and don't be forlorn.
Be proud of your existence, you're somebody you are.
Look up at the sky, you'll see me. I'm a star.
Proud to be a father, your lover and a friend,
We knew that sometime, later, now, it all had to end.
Think of me kindly, my integrity was sound
Think of me often, let my love abound.
Never was a poet, gentle, and sometimes wise,
Like so many others, never got first prize.
Remember what I told you, friends are everything,
Even at a time like this, they take away the sting.
Things are left unspoken, that's probably the best
You have to sit where they have sat, and then, you can rest.
Country line, and tenpin, fishing and DIY,
Are the pastimes I will miss, when I eventually die,
Now of course it's happened, at last you are alone,
I'm sorry that I left you, cannot fax or phone,
Please be strong my darlings, enjoy life while you can,
Our lives, our deaths, are part of God's eternal plan.

Oh To Be A Poet

QUIET REFLECTIONS 1999

Oh, to be a poet, to right wrongs with ones phrases,
To create colours with chosen words
Be able to douse big blazes.
To wallow, in perfect English, put tears in people's eyes,
Be capable of timeless work,
Be specific, and be wise.
Oh, to be a poet, alert senses, bring big smiles,
Be creative, teach the world to sing
Enhance with words, what others would defile.
Oh to be linguistic, full of English prose,
Adored by readers, kissed by praise,
Let them smell an English rose.
Use a thousand letters, miles of flowing text,
Construct villanelles and rondeaus
Let them say, 'what ever's coming next?'
Oh to be a poet, who cares, who loves, who thinks,
Who reaches out to common folk,
Who created thirst, lets peoples drink.
Choose words, paint pretty pictures, state your case,
Indulge the human brain,
Oh to be a poet, let people know your face.

Forgive And Forget

PROGRESSIVE THOUGHTS 1999

Bitterness wanes,
Priorities change,
Too busy to let it hurt,
The laws advice
Gave them no choice
Made history seem very curt.
To forgive and forget,
Live and let live
Is much harder said, than done
Let evil dwell
Should be in hell
It seems like the villain won.
Lots of people,
Lots to forget,
Loving not a strong trait,
Can we forgive?
Can we let live?
The world might have a long wait.
Mostly we're sad,
When things go bad,
But revenge makes matters worse,
Turn your cheek
Be strong and meek
Let love put the world in reverse.

My Special Place

SO DEAR TO MY HEART 2000

I can see a special place,
It's a picture n my mind,
Where trees and shrubs are everywhere
And people are so kind.
A little church nestles in the trees,
The bells are always ringing.
Where violence and crime are gone,
And children are always singing.
There are no locks on any doors,
Law and order reigns.
Where there is truly peace on earth.
No noisy cars or planes.
A little girl walks down the road,
Holding an old mans hand.
She should be playing with her friends,
But she learns and understands.
Harmony exists in church and home,
Where caring and friendship's sought,
Where lethal weapons do not exist
Where battles are never fought.
It only ever rains at night,
The rivers are never dry,
Where natures balance is stabilised,
Where salmon jump, and eagles fly.
The sound of laughter fills the air,
Children play and parents care.
Old people have no fear, and dread,
There are no poor and life is fair.

Mystery

RHYMING TIMES 1999

There's an eerie chill in the manor house,
The upstairs room is gloomy and so damp.
An uneasy mood to frighten a mouse,
Not even homely for a vagrant tramp.
What happened in this tall grey dwelling?
That keeps away bats and nosey parkers.
Black magic powers or hideous killing,
That makes the cold night even darker.
A mystery to scare the strongest stomach
A torture room, screams and wails in the night
Or a hairy monster, with crooked back,
A long dangling cobweb puts you to flight.
If you are curious, just listen to me,
Walk straight passed, and go home to tea

The Dancers

SEARCHING INSPIRATIONS 1999

Majestic in motion, sensual, when still.
Gracefully synchronised, a task to fulfil.
Beautifully rhythmic, they mimic the beat,
So perfectly matched, the world at their feet.
Spanish like beauty, her gown in a twirl,
Professional performance, from such a young girl,
Marble like aura, with a feint tinge of pink.
Adrenalin pumping, more than you think.
Are they in love, he holds her with grace,
The special eye contact, the smile on her face,
The music is wonderful, enhancing the dance
They deserve gold, can they take the chance.
They're actually older, than their actions tell,
He's tall and handsome, and she is his belle,
Their elegant grace outweighs their wealth
For they are a statue, on our bedroom shelf.
White opaque crystal, a light shining down,
Removes any movement, or musical sound.
The couple stand poised to begin their dance.
I have imagined this gold medal chance.

Hypothesising

WORDS IN HARMONY 2000

"If you could have your life again, and make a change at all"
Is a burning question, in my mind, looking back when I was small.
Why was I born in thirty nine, and not in eighty four.
I wouldn't be very old, and maybe not so poor.
Why was I born in Hampshire, and not in the south of Spain,
I might have been a pirate, and sailed the Spanish main.
I could have danced Flamenco, or faced a raging bull.
Instead I work for a pump firm, and drive to work from Poole.
I could have had rich parents, been born with a silver spoon,
I might have been a Lord, by now, or perhaps been to the moon.
But we lived in a railway house, where the windows always rattled
When the mail train went through, early, and neighbours tittle tattled
Why was I born so healthy, and christened, another Brian,
Why did I go to Grammar school, and have to keep on trying,
If I had lived in America, I would not have met my wife,
I would have driven a Chrysler, had a very different life.
I would not have had my children, or friends, that I hold dear.
I might not have spoken English, or had a pin of beer,
I could have been a gipsy, or an orphan, or a mute,
It's fun to hypothesise, but I was dealt this suit.

Ode From A Foot

AN ECHO OF POETS 2000

The weight I support is amazing,
Sometimes I feel I'm a-blazing.
Without my support, she's a little bit short,
I wish she would do some lazing.
Just out of bed, I am happy,
On the carpet, my toes are all flappy.
Ready for work, pulls me up with a jerk,
I am laced up tight by a nappy.
My bottom is hot and quite tender,
No matter, what my gender.
My skin gets all hard, I might need a guard,
She needs someone to befriend her.
I need someone to look after my list,
I need Julie, my chiropodist.
She washes me down, with a smile, not a frown
And I feel like I just had a kiss.
With care she scrapes off my skin,
It really makes me feel thin,
It's corny I know, but the lumps have to go
And I know I've been done by a pro.
My talons are discoloured and long,
She clips them and never goes wrong.
The quicks are all clean, my digits feel lean
And the cleaners got rid of the pong.
She cares for my feet, like a nurse,
When she's finished she gets out my purse
At five pounds a foot, she'll soon have loot
Then she'll not appear, and I'll curse

The Grocery Round

UNDERNEATH THE STARS 2004

We needed the money, my dad was gone
Mum worked in the local grocery store.
They wanted a young lad to deliver the goods
I got a bike, five bob, and nothing more.
The carrier was on the handle bars,
All that weight to turn and steer,
For three old pence you could buy a mars
We sold lemonade, but not canned beer.
They sent me out in storm, wind, and rain.
To Park gates east, and Branksome Park
Every Friday night, and Saturday again.
through remote woods, to houses dark,
I climbed the stairs in blocks of flats,
Soaked to the skin, or sweating like hell.
Carrying boxes, higher than my hat
Struggling with my elbow, to ring the bell.
I hated the dark, the wet, and the cold
Tripping on logs, old carpets, and steps,
Getting rude comments, 'you're late', I'm told,
Smelling old cat's food, but had no regrets,
Helped old ladies, called back with the lard,
Got a sweet or two from aged gents,
Sang at their socials, it was quite hard,
It helped our family, and was well meant.

The Call Of Morning

A MOMENT OF DEJA VU 2007

As a summer dawn leads on another day,
In the eerie still of this busy world,
A blackbird sings to awaken me.
Like a sentinel on neighbourhood watch.
From his favourite position high in the apple tree
Searching the scales, like a novice singer.
Almost melancholy, he triples and rolls,
Never repeating, a volley of notes randomly sung.
It's four in the morning, the world is still.
Far away in the distance, almost an echo,
Another sentinel joins in the chorus.
Some house sparrows, now twittering
Their new brood is hungry.
An old wood pigeon starts to warble
The world is awakening to another day
There is nothing on earth which stimulates so,
The soul renewed, and regenerated by this music.
Music to our ears, gentle unchained melody
Fit for a king, orchestrated by God,
A feeling of warmth and relaxation,
To see us through, another busy day.

The Robin

FAMILY MATTERS

Ever since her mother died, my wife has had a hunch,
That a robin, in our garden, is her mother come for lunch
This may seem rather strange, but wherever we make our home
This little bunch of joy, won't leave us alone.
We recently moved, to spend our latter years
It was only two days before he reappeared
Even when you speak to him, he never flies away
He cocks his head and looks at us, we think he's here to stay
I walked into my tool shed to put some things away
And now he's in there nesting, busy all the day.
I have had to cut an access hole, so he can come and go
When I lock up the shed at night, and he just seemed to know
I hope it is mums spirit, she was really good to me,
It may just be our fantasy, but we must wait and see.
When she died, we rushed to her never got to say goodbye
So maybe she has taken flight, and come to live nearby

A Quiet Longing, 2008

BEST POEMS & POETS 2007

Whilst sunning myself in the garden
Enjoying the solitude of the fall
I can listen to the sound of the noisy world
Which makes one feel very small
Though no one can see me writing
Huge jet planes are passing by
The main road is busy with speeding cars
People movement is very high.
What am I doing? Why am I here?
The time the days move fast
Everyone's in a hurry, it seems
But for all, the die is cast
The sun is still shining, in October
It feels like a summers day
Global warming has come to town
But the noise won't go away
I'm sure we all long for some slowing down
The comforting clip clop of hooves
Creaky carts, abandoned roads,
And a quieter laid back mode.

It's A Mystery

THE BEST POETS 2007

I don't understand what life is about,
It's a mystery, with loads of doubt.
A life begins, too young to know,
Dressed to kill, put on show.
Marmite soldiers, porridge and cake,
Food to eat, a mess to make.
Suddenly you know some stuff
Mum's kind, but Nan's bear is rough,
Things to learn, really quite quick,
Behave yourself, mind the bamboo stick.
Of to school, short trousers, cap
You don't know this is the first lap.
Silly games, hop scotch, and touch
I never liked cold weather mush,
Chased the girls, kissed one or two
They were different, not like you
Passed my test, did exams
Went to Weymouth and saw the trams
Suddenly I am in the choir,
They all could sing, but I sang higher
Now I'm someone, have respect.
Discovered girls, went out and necked,
They were different, but smelt so nice,
Would they become my only vice?
Most of my family were women,
My best friend died, that's an omen,
I've been happy, then sad
I was sorry, then glad
What does our life really mean?

Weddings and funerals I've seen
Ballroom dancing was next
Hard steps made me vexed
Met a gorgeous girl with charm
Waltzed, held her in my arms
Felt something new, magic
Would this all end up tragic
I had three or four friends
Held hands kissed, no loose ends
This was it, love was real
Something warm, I could feel
Learned how to give,
Learned how to live,
Life is a mystery, living is love
Lost more friends, to heaven above.
Cried buckets, was sad
Had Babies, was glad
Miracles happen, life is a yoyo
Sometimes you're up, then you're low
A roller coaster of sadness and joy
Death if a friend, birth if a boy
God wants us to be happy
God invented the dirty nappy
God wants us to know real sadness
Then we'll know real gladness
I'd be dubious if faith was simple
Mystery is like a baby's dimple
I love my friends, I love my life
I love to laugh, I love my wife
Life is a mystery, discover why

Something Wonderful

FORWARD PRESS POETS

I wanted to write something wonderful
To celebrate, two decades of verse
Something triumphant, no praise is enough
For an anthology in which to immerse.
The hundreds of writers of which I am one
Are so grateful to be part of this theme
Press forward I say, we can write every day
Because we are truly part of this team.
It's wonderful to have such an anchor
With strong roots on which to improve
We want poetry now and forever
Easy to read, but truly in the grove.
I am nearing my personal century
Published poems from the heart
It is truly something wonderful, magic
To write, to be read, to be part.
Let's have a huge celebration
Let's love reading the written word
Let's spread love and peace forever
For the pen is, mightier than the sword.

Spring In My Garden 2008

LIFES SERENITIES

I'm looking out the window,
And spring is almost here
Our Camellias are showing off
The daffodil yellow shines clear.
The buds are popping in the copse
Making the shrubs more dense,
We've blue tits in the nesting box,
And the robins on the fence
The magpies nest is occupied.
The squirrels on the feed
The air is fresh the grass is green
What more do we need?
All the roses are budding up
The climbers standing tall
Suddenly the forsythia's out
And spring is on the ball

Boundaries 2008

THE ART OF LIFE

Our lives are controlled by boundaries,
these are the limits of our lives.
How far we can hit a ball
Or, legally how fast can we drive
These are almost unwritten byelaws
A cultural rule to survive
How we can control our children
How can they live, free and thrive.
Sensible parameters, working rules, as such
Though these are ignored by children
Different families have different views
,and these cause problems, often
Boundaries aren't meant to be bent or moved
They're in place as basic guidelines
They aren't meant to be legal laws
But used wisely, by peoples minds
A hedge of laurel's a boundary
A parental rule equally so.
It's a form of safety regulation
Which can be adjusted as we go.
A 'freedom' to be yet limiting, see
I can do this, but I shouldn't do that
We can have rules, which are used as tools
You can have sweets if you feed the cat
Boundaries are meant, as a sign of love
For peoples safety in a a dangerous time
Fast cars can kill, paedophiles strike
Our lovely world is no longer sublime.

Children, please listen to what mum says
This life's not a trial run.
One silly mistake, can mean an unhappy life
So listen, be safe, and have fun.

Our Grandaughter

FAMILY AND FRIENDS

We miss you more than words can say,
Two thousand miles away, on holiday.
We thought that we would never meet,
We love the patter of your little feet.
Thank you Ollie for enriching our life,
You are an absolute delight.
From the start, we named you Angel Eyes,
Blond, curly hair, and full of surprise.
We love you lots, and always will.
So well brought up, our lives you fill.
'Olivia' just hovers on the breeze,
And Rose is nannies name, she is so pleased,
that you are happy to be with us,
Our lovely Ollie, who makes no fuss.
We wish you a long and happy life,
You're adorable, a little wife,
Busy cleaning, and tidying up.
Uh-ooh nanny, I've knocked my cup.
You light up my house, when you come to call,
You're big in our house, even though you're small.
We'll bring you something nice from Crete
Our little Ollie with the dancing feet.

My Love It's Poetry

SWEET NOTHINGS

I am lost in a dream of romantic bliss,
Where nothing's forbidden, especially a kiss.
Where the world stays outside, and love stays within,
and lovers sweat together, skin to skin.
My sweetheart is gorgeous, sensual and kind.
Locked in a relationship where love is blind.
She dresses to kill, and likes to be admired.
Legs like an angel, and a body inspired.
This is not real, is it? Can it be true?
A lover, a friend, designed just for you.
Is this a soul mate, who loves me to death.
She is so close to me, I can feel her breath.
Am I dreaming, when she graces the hall
"Hello my darling, I forgot to call,"
"to tell you I love you, with all my heart"
"I hope and pray, that we're never apart.
I am so lucky, to have found someone,
Someone like my love, who is lots of fun.
Compatible loving, so tender and sweet,
My lover, my wife who makes my heart beat.

Catch Me When I Fall 2008

Through the trials and tribulations
Of this earthly life's' hard call
There's that lovely family feeling
That they'll catch you if you fall

It stems from mothers heartbeat,
And fathers strong warm arms
Feelings never spoken about
They'll not let you come to harm.
Sometimes it's almost E.S.P
Parents sense where dangers lurk.
Being aware, just taking care
It's a recipe that works
Knocks and bumps, scratched elbows
Plasters on kids heads
Holding out strong loving hands
Bathing, and warm beds.
These early knocks so important
When later in your life
Personal tragedies do unfold
That cause us untold strife.
Serious accidents, untimely deaths
Rock us badly, break our hearts.
Make us feel our worlds will end
Because we thought we'd never part.
It's then we recall these feelings
I am sure we all have felt
When loved ones cast their earthly mould

And we wish our hearts could melt.
Be thankful for your anchor
In case sadness should you befall
And pray that loving family arms,
Will catch you when you fall

Chapter 5

War

Memories

TEARS OF WAR 1998

I can remember being four, looking up at my dad,
He'd just lost a leg in France, but didn't look too bad.
I thought he was enormous, when I was two foot six,
He stood there in his khaki, supported by two sticks.
I was born in thirty nine, three months into the war,
But being so young at the time, it didn't leave a scar.
I can still see the black out blinds, the bed under the stairs,
And hear the air raid siren, that haunting sound, that scares.
I remember 'D' Day, but I didn't know at the time,
Why so many planes flew overhead, blocking out the sky.
There were so many different ones, they just kept coming, more and more
Black, small profiles in the sky, like a carpet on a floor.
We played with old 'ration books', cut tickets for the bus,
Played hide and seek with Barbara, my cousin lived with us.
The men had signed up, gone to war, we had to cut our bills.
Candlesticks, and small coal fires, thick blankets and no frills.
Suddenly, I went to school, the war was running on,
We had milk, and short bread biscuits, my dad, he was already gone.
Food was scarce, no butter, but beef dripping on our toast,
Lots of Spam, and powdered egg, but, we did have Sunday roast.
Then the war was over, the Andersons pulled down,
There was one string of German bombs, dropped on Bournemouth town.
I saw my first banana, this was 1948,
Then I met my new step dad, my mum had a new mate.

We had no separate bathroom, no hot water tank,
In a tin bath, in the scullery, on Friday night, we sank.
The rent man usually called, when I was in the nude,
Back door open, bacon on, it was all fairly crude.

Casualties Of War—A Villanelle

POETIC DESIGNS 2004

Were we destined to be starving and poor?
We are bony, thin, and have no shirts,
Is this the life we were looking for?
Walking has made our limbs, tired, and sore,
It's so very hard, walking in mud and dirt,
Were we destined to be starving and poor?
Thousands fleeing, from the bloody war,
The refugees camp bustling, alert,
Is this the life we were looking for?
We've lost half our village, maybe more,
Some just died of fright, many badly hurt,
Were we destined to be starving and poor?
Hoping our neighbours will open their doors,
Political situation is strangely inert,
Is this the life we were looking for?
Anymore rain, we'll be down on the floor,
We've no energy left that we can exert,
Were we destined to be starving and poor
Is this the life we were looking for?

The Battlefield

POPPY FIELDS 2007

Is it time to die in this awful place?
I have just seen death on a soldiers face.
Lying here, bleeding, terrified, cold,
With death all around it's hard to be bold.
Pandemonium everywhere, horrendous noise,
Life hangs in the balance, for us soldier boys
Deafening thuds, machine guns and mines,
Mayhem, and bloodshed, amidst our lines.
Keep your head down, catching your breath,
We are inches away, from maiming or death.
Terrible screams, amidst shell bursts and sand,
Black smoke, and mist, some ones dead hand.
Sharp metal objects, barbed wire and stakes
Pinned down in hell, machine gun rakes,
Got to get out of this, or die on the way
Fighting for freedom, on this terrible day.
Young men crying, thousands lay dead,
Human stupidity, it has to be said,
Was I born to a world, that now wishes me dead?
My wife so worried, in tears on the bed.
God help me, and the rest of my troop
We have got to get moving, try and regroup.
Backed up from the sea, by navy shells
I'm creeping forward, hoping all will be well.
A headless body, a soldier screams now
Keep moving soldier, we'll survive somehow
A breach in the wall, a way through, at last
On your feet lads, and run bloody fast.

The Colour Of War

HEROES 2010

The world needs heroes and we need ours, so many brave men die, hour by hour.

Fighting for a cause, so far from home, willing to die, like the legions of Rome.

Unorthodox battles, against ambushing foes. Threatening world peace, they have to go.

Britain and America, hand in glove, in a bloody conflict with no loss of love.

More than war, where poppies grow. to help the Afghans, stem the flow.

Difficult terrain, hostile, severe, costing our courageous men, so dear.

The world must help, it's a dangerous place. The enemy frightened to show their face.

The fight must go on, we must not lose. We must eliminate terrorist crews.

If there is one God, what is it about? Our way of life, some niggling doubts.

Our armed forces must be backed. Bloodied, injured, no courage lacked.

Against extremists, of course we are, We need a future, to know where we are.

Create a future for our kin. Pave the way, with love, not sin.

God bless our men, who front the line. Who risk their lives, and do not whine.

They are all worth their weight in gold. for standing strong, and being bold.

9/11 should have shown this world, what terrorism can unfurl.
Then London, Baghdad, it had to end. They have to know we'll never bend.
Mothers weep, and wives lament, Grieving families feel the dent.
So may good people, paying the price. to finance someone else's vice.

Love In War

VOICE IN THE SILENCE

Through time in memorial
True love has been
The bonus, the prize
Or the death of we
People who live
With their hearts
Or their heads
Finding a hard way
To pick up life's threads
Causing mayhem, or war
For a damsel they saw
Risking their lives
For love, or for wives
A first kiss may be pure,
But never the cure
Sons were a must
Through love, or through lust
To finance an army
Which can drive you barmy
Love is the splendour
Love is the drive
Consummate quickly
Whilst you're still alive
Love can be wonderful
Love can be strong
But statistically
It's, never for long.
Too many enemies,
Plotting their cause.

Happy to fondle,
With their blood claws
Breaking up families,
So torn apart
Causing such hatred
To tear out a heart
So there you have it
Love in war
Was it all worth it?
The bed, or the sword

The Morning After 2007

I've worked all night, it's six in the morn,
Now I can't recognise where I was born.
The Junkers came under the cranes last night,
Blew off the roof, the moon was bright
We ran for the shelters, but not much good,
Bombs killed twelve people where they stood.
The naval factory took it hard,
A dangerous place, the old dockyard.
I've finished my shift making submarine parts
The bombings stopped now, it is night when it starts.
My bikes still intact, take it out of the rack,
I'll be so glad to hit the sack.
Outside the gates now, where is the road?
Suddenly my heart has a heavy load.
The houses are gone, there's one hell of a mess,
Fire and dust, and one road less.
Piles of rubble, as far as you look.
How many lives have the Nazis took?
I need to get home, I'm worried for mum
I hope she's alive, she'll be hoping I come
Not much left of the old Baptist church
The spires still there, but it looks on the lurch.
There's a massive bang, as I fight my way through
A timed land mine waiting, and it just blew.
It's lifted the spire, clean off the ground
When the dust settles, there's a huge rubble mound
My God, that was close, it's terrible here,
I'm tired and weary, with pains in my ears.
My wife is probably at her wits end,
The babe will be crying, it's hard, don't pretend.
We must get out of this dangerous town

I'll take my family to Wallisdown
I'll ask the boss, if I can leave,
There's a setters vacancy, I believe.
No one is safe, many friends dead
Crushed or blown up, or hit on the head.
Pandemonium in old Portsmouth town
Great big craters, whole areas down
I'm hungry as hell, not feeling well
A long way home through the smoke and the smell
I can here the sea, I'm at Eastern road
Not too far now from Highgrove road.
Thank God it's Friday, a day of rest
I'll do the garden, give it my best.
I drop my bike, inside the gate
Nice to be home but it's getting late.
"Hello, love" Where have you been?"
She'd tears in her eyes" You hadn't been seen"
"It's Saturday now, we thought we'd lost you"
"twenty four hours, you've been overdue"
"Thank God you are safe, I'll get you some tea"
"I'm so very happy, you've come home to me

Chapter 6

Travel

I Wonder?

TO WHOM IT MAY CONCERN 1998

Hello, to someone in a far off place,
We don't know each other, I've not seen your face.
The message is in English, can you understand?
What is your name ? Where is your land?
I've often wondered who's out there you see,
With a wife, and children, happy like me.
Not all the world wants fighting, and war,
We'd rather be friendly, have peace ever more.
Buenos dies, bonjour, just hello,
We're farther North, are you below?
Are you a reader, a writer, or such ?
Could you reply? If so thank you so much.
I married my wife a long time ago,
You cant love a person, you don't even know.
We didn't meet foreigners, back in those days,
I always regretted those limiting ways.
As an industrial nation, we have fax and phone,
Power and fuel, but everyone moans.
Maybe you are luckier, on your little isle,
Where the sun shines bright, and everything's wild
Please find a way, translate if you can,
Get to fax/phone, and we'll make a plan.
If you can't read, the future looks bleak,
Let's hope you re-float it and the bottle don't leak.
The Earth is spherical, and rotates once a day,
Two thirds is water, and you're far away,
The British isles is a speck on the chart,
This bottles been lucky, or fate gave it heart.

Our Island Home

TURNING EMOTIONS 1999

The grass is always greener, on this precious island home,
We should count our blessings, no matter where we may roam,
Our Mother earth is wonderful, fantastic sights to see,
The Rocky mountains, endless pines, spell freedom for me.
We strolled the sun baked shores of Rhodes, have eaten feta cheese
Swam amongst the shoals of fish, sampled sunburnt knees,
Glided up the Eiffel Tower, gasped at matchbox cars
Lazed on a sandy Corfu beach, and gazed up at the stars.
Moonlight nights, fabulous sights, are the same the world over
But there's nothing like a balmy English day, hunting a four leaf clover.
Floodlit Stirling Castle, is a calming sight for me,
It beckons me to my hotel, for a red hot cup of tea.
Monte Carlo water front, with its 'copter pad, and pool,
Impress us folk from colder climes, it's an energy renewal.
Unless, you've spent a sunny day, on the rolling planes of Wilts
Or relaxed, in Bournemouth Square, watching Highlanders in kilts.
This fertile land we live in, should satisfy our dreams
Watch the boats in Dartmouth, and taste some Devon cream
Waterfalls and mill streams, the babbling is relaxing
Watching brown trout rise for flies, is not exactly taxing
Our rolling seas, and rocky coasts, emphasise our island status
Reminding us we're safe and free to eat cold lunch with lettuce
Our island home is our safe house, our anchor and our life
Safer, with our 'protocol', than Africa's violent strife.
We have to see the turmoil, to appreciate our land
Walk forward, with stability, love and peace, go hand in hand.

WHERE THE HEART IS 2000

When I was young, I thought that fishing was a waste of time.
I'd walked the shore, seen angled rods from me to Durley chine.
Studying rod tips, shelling limpets, staring out to sea.
Never saw one catch a fish, from dinner time to tea.
Retired couples dragging dogs, or running to keep up,
The worst for chucking sand about were yappy little pups.
You cock your leg against my rod, I'll make you bloody bark,"
"I'll tie you to my great big hook, and feed you to the shark,"
One day my dad hooked a bass, in a very heavy swell.
Excitement, yes, a gleaming fish, and I was hooked as well.
I bought this rod, big it was, all of nine feet long,
Not a clue, solid glass, but it was very strong.
Many a night I stood there, trying to see the tip,
Night time plays some funny tricks, so I bought a bell and clip.
Had a bite didn't remove it, as I oughta,
Struck hard, damn, it flew off, and landed in the water.
Had some good days, lots more bad, never caught a twenty pounder.
A small sole here, a small skate there, sometimes caught a flounder.
One night caught no fish at all, but, went home with a duck,
Next week just up the road, I caught a rabbit buck.
I've been in the rough water after floats,
Stood in Poole Harbour, in a great fishing coat.
Once I came home soaking wet, in my soggy undies,
Sometimes, went out on Friday night, and came back home on Sunday.
I've seen sunset on the Purbeck hills, sunrise over Wight.
Chased mice along the shingle, seen some wondrous sights,
Fishing s a sporting pastime, packed with natures ways
Tiddlers, crabs, no fish at all, I loved my fishing days.

The Lake

PERCEPTIONS 2001

The crystal waters lap the shore
Its calmness is serene,
The shoreline sharply contrasts
With mountain wall, and cypress green.
Startling beauty makes you gasp,
Tones grey to sparkling white
Flecks of faun and orange,
Lakes surface, glimmering bright.
Wild fowl graze so happily here,
Ecology supporting well,
Food for birds and fish alike,
In, this quiet lakeside swell.
The vastness of this waterway,
Exceeds our wildest dreams,
Cool and clear and crystal like,
Fed by a mountain stream.

TAKE A MOMENT 2004

The calm green waters, reflecting the sun,
Hundreds of sun seekers, looking for fun.
A watery paradise, in a picturesque cove,
Spectacular cliffs, contrasting above.
A fine sandy beach, curving down to the sea,
Zebra like sunshades to protect you and me.
A cliff set restaurant, commanding the view
Ham and cheese rolls or a hot fishy stew.
A white glistening catamaran, fully rigged out,
All the crew members, on the lookout.
Wonderful colours, quilting the scope.
Happy people, laughing with holiday hopes.
Calm waters broken by white rolling wakes,
Speed boats and dinghies, without any brakes.
A whole coastal area bustling with noise,
Children laughing, girls, chasing boys
Small coloured triangles covering white,
Brown and pink flesh, bonding the sight.
Tall dark pine trees, breaking the light,
Lovely cool shade, and no breeze to bite,
A wonderful ambiance, so beautiful here,
Ristorante, so full, clinking glasses of beer,
No one could wish for more heaven than this
Warm sun, cool sea, this is holiday bliss.

The Choice Is Yours

LIFES WONDERS

Capital cities are all very well,
But they're noisy, bustling and sometimes smell.
Despite the crowds, they are lonely places,
Big shops, traffic and foreign faces,
Probably the loneliest streets on earth,
Faceless people, and not much mirth.
Roaring traffic horns and buses,
Rubbish strewn and everyone rushes
The rolling hills are a very different choice
The birds all sing, with familiar voice
Views for miles, peace on earth,
Solitary trees, with enormous girth,
Alone, but not lonely, so much to embrace
Smells of harvest, by god's good grace.
Silence is golden, the busy sky blue,
Quiet contentment, for me and you.
The world's your oyster
The choice there for all
Go where your'e happy
Whatever the call
The call maybe city, office is there
Difficult location but family needs care
Earning big money, important role,
It may not last, but better than dole.
If country life draws you, then you have the choice
Live in the valley, where you hear your voice
Life seems much slower, more peace and calm
Work longer hours, when you're down on the farm.

Heavens In Your Mind

AN ODE TO OPTIMISM

The glistening turquoise waters, glided quietly towards the shore.
The tiny, foamy waves lapped gently on to the sand, asking for more.
The Cyprus sun, high above the wispy clouds, lit up the coral sands,
Casting short shadows, under the colourful, flapping, sun shades.
Despite the background sound of sleepy waves,
And a barely audible chatter, the silence was almost golden.
On the blue, blue sky, small fluffy clouds eased across the view
Contrasting, with the turquoise sea.
Hidden rocks, and marine weeds, made mysterious shadowy stripes,
In the shallows, of the crystal waters.
New visitors, undressed, fidgeted, and gazed around,
At all this, astonishingly, natural beauty.
It is a warm, and golden day.
To the East, the huge man made structures, changed the horizon,
Forward in time, to now.
Hundreds of tiny balconies, small windows, and strategically placed plants
Built to give contrasts, of pink to white, and various greens.
A hauntingly beautiful place, here, in modern times.
Scattered with tall palms, and tiny coloured triangles,
Barely covering sun worshippers.
A moving panoramic view, of a historically magnificent coast,
Haunted by Aphrodites' ghost.
A very apt parallel, there is a God.
Nothing, so beautiful could be created by man, could it?
You see, there is a heaven on earth.
It's only in ones mind.
May be your heaven is just different from mine?
But beautiful and almost holy to you.

Imagine This

MY WORDS ARE MY VOICE

Imagine a place, with a white frozen lake,
Long freezing icicles hanging from rails.
Cold ruddy faces of bustling skaters,
Brightly dressed girls, and heavier males.
Imagine Canada geese, slipping and sliding,
Mallard ducks curious, the water won't drip.
The small yachts suspended, solid in place
The wintery cold has the south in it's grip.
Now the small streams are babbling again,
The frost has departed, the thaw is alive.
The new energy of Spring, rejuvenates life,
Fledglings and offspring all set to thrive.
Imagine soft golden sands, nine miles long,
Safe bathing beaches, and blue flag seas.
Thousands of tourists seeking the sun,
Basking and enjoying the balmy breeze.
Dream about unbelievably beautiful scenes,
Lush green fields, and expansive views.
Wild deer foraging in forests so dense,
Sunsets of soft pink and orange hues.
Just visit us here, in the beautiful South.
Magnificent hotels, even caravan parks.
Something for everyone here in Bournemouth
Our wild Dorset coves, helps us make a mark.

Corfu In The Sun

CAPTURED CREATIVITY 2010

The morning sunlight radiates through,
ventilation slats, on the floor near you.
A bright new day is born.
The summer heat brightens the balcony,
The vast matt sky, like the blue nowhere,
Stunning in its mere existence,
Creates a backdrop for the view.
Shadowy, greyish, green mountains,
Lush green hillsides of olive and cypress trees
Indescribable beauty for me and you.
No traffic noise, no clock chimes,
Just a wonderful silence,
Broken by the different sounds of birds,
In this huge expanse, of green, lush wild fields.
The breeze gently moving tiny leaves
On soft new green foliage.
A lonely cottage, half hidden by wild scrub,
Red roofed and cream,
Increases the feeling of quiet solitude.
Time ticking by, unrushed by human frailty.
A slight sensation of water lapping,
In the glistening, flat blue Complex pool.
Light dancing on its surface,
Moving but almost noiseless,
The occasional bird flitting between feeding and nest
The world's wonders, the absolute best